COCKCROW TO STARLIGHT

A Day Full of Poetry

*Also available by Rumer Godden
in Macmillan Children's Books*

Candy Floss & Impunity Jane
Mr McFadden's Hallowe'en
The Diddakoi
A Kindle of Kittens
The Old Woman Who Lived in a Vinegar Bottle
Mouse Time
Thursday's Children
Listen to the Nightingale
Premlata and the Festival of Lights

and

Prayers from the Ark
*translated from the French
Poems by Carmen Bernos de Gasztold*

COCKCROW TO STARLIGHT

A Day Full of Poetry

CHOSEN BY
RUMER GODDEN

ILLUSTRATED BY
MAGGIE KNEEN

MACMILLAN CHILDREN'S BOOKS

First published 1996 by Macmillan Children's Books

This edition published 1997 by Macmillan Children's Books
a division of Macmillan Publishers Limited
25 Eccleston Place, London SW1W 9NF
and Basingstoke

Associated companies throughout the world

ISBN 0 330 34302 5

9 8 7 6 5 4 3

A CIP catalogue record for this book is available from
the British Library.

Typeset by Intype, London
Printed and bound in Great Britain by Mackays of Chatham plc, Kent

"Do your best to hoard up whatever you can in that little bookcase of your mind: you want to fill it as full as possible."

From a letter written by St Thomas Aquinas to one of his students in 1270

Introduction

Poetry is not something far away from you; it is made of the stuff of every day. If you are a poet, you may write a poem about anything from a rose to a mountain, from a cat to your roller-skates, because poetry tells about things in a way more beautiful or more ugly, more exciting, more glad or more sad than ordinary writing and talking. It is more memorable too, because it is in rhythm – it is the rhythm that makes it poetry.

Contents

COCKLIGHT

The Prayer of the Cock CARMEN BERNOS
    DE GASZTOLD *translated by Rumer Godden* 3
A Day (extract) EMILY DICKINSON 3
The Dustman CLIVE SAMSON 4
Night Mail (extract) W. H. AUDEN 4
Minnie and Winnie ALFRED, LORD TENNYSON 6
The Fifteen Acres JAMES STEPHENS 7
Shock-headed Peter HEINRICH HOFFMANN 9
I'd Love to be a Fairy's Child ROBERT GRAVES 10
Pippa Passes ROBERT BROWNING 10

BREAKFAST AND OUT OF DOORS

A Thanksgiving to God ROBERT HERRICK 13
Cows JAMES REEVES 14
The King's Breakfast A. A. MILNE 15
Madam Eglantine (extract) GEOFFREY CHAUCER 19
Alas! Alack! WALTER DE LA MARE 20

Out of Doors (extract) WILLIAM WORDSWORTH 21
The Rain MAY JUSTUS 21
Nine-o'Clock Bell ELEANOR FARJEON 22

SCHOOL MORNING

Piping Down the Valleys Wild WILLIAM BLAKE 25
Words (extract) ELEANOR FARJEON 26
Exercise Book JACQUES PREVERT 27
   translated by Paul Dehn
I'm Nobody EMILY DICKINSON 29
Lincoln NANCY BYRD TURNER 30
Jazz Fantasia CARL SANDBERG 31
I Had a Little Nut-tree TRADITIONAL 32
The Pied Piper (extract) ROBERT BROWNING 33

LUNCH BREAK

Chips STANLEY COOK 37
Miss T. WALTER DE LA MARE 38
Skipping Song JOHN WALSH 39
Playground Rhymes TRADITIONAL 40
Laura JEFF MOSS 42
My True Love IVY O. EASTWICK 42
Under the Greenwood Tree WILLIAM SHAKESPEARE 44
Cabin Boy CARYL BRAHMS 45
Childhood SIR THOMAS MORE 46

SCHOOL AFTERNOON

The Rugger Match (extract) SIR JOHN SQUIRE   49
Pincushion Song ROBERT GRAVES   50
Things Men Have Made D. H. LAWRENCE   51
How to Paint the Portrait of a Bird JACQUES PREVERT   52
   translated by Paul Dehn
Computer JAMES SUTHERLAND, aged 11   54
Romance W. J. TURNER   55
The Ballad of the Kon-Tiki (extract) IAN SERRAILLIER   57
Le Hibou et la Poussiquette *translated by*   59
   Francis Steegmuller
The Owl and the Pussycat EDWARD LEAR   60
School's Out W. H. DAVIES   62

PLAYTIME

Tom-Tom (extract) PHYLLIS McGINLEY   65
One Star Less RUSSELL HOBAN   67
Catch ELEANOR FARJEON   67
Jesse James (extract) WILLIAM ROSE BENET   69
The Runaway ROBERT FROST   71
A Boy Fishing E. SCOVELL   72
The Doll House (extract) PHYLLIS McGINLEY   73
Allie ROBERT GRAVES   75

TEATIME, SUPPERTIME AND PETS

Tea in a Space Ship JAMES KIRKUP   79
Beautiful Soup LEWIS CARROLL   81
A Ternarie of Littles ROBERT HERRICK   82
Everyone has Gone to Town (extract) FREDEGOND   83
    SHOVE
Thy Servant a Dog RUDYARD KIPLING   84
Beth Gêlert (extract) WILLIAM ROBERT SPENCER   85
Guinea Pigs RUMER GODDEN   88
Autumn Evening FRANCES CORNFORD   89

TWILIGHT AND STORIES OUT
OF THIS WORLD

Dream Song WALTER DE LA MARE   93
Little Orphant Annie JAMES WHITCOMB RILEY   94
Adventures of Isabel OGDEN NASH   95
Overheard on a Saltmarsh HAROLD MUNRO   97
The Wraggle Taggle Gypsies UNKNOWN   98
The Queen of Sheba's Gifts OSBERT SITWELL   100
Pegasus HENRY WADSWORTH LONGFELLOW   101
To Night (extract) PERCY BYSSHE SHELLEY   103
Collective Nouns CHRISTOPHER HASSALL   104

IN THE NIGHT

Night WILLIAM BLAKE   107

The Starlight Night (extract) GERARD MANLEY   109
  HOPKINS

Star Wish TRADITIONAL   109

Lady Moon CHRISTINA ROSSETTI   110

Fairies' Lullaby for Titania WILLIAM SHAKESPEARE   110

Hiawatha's Childhood (extract) HENRY WADSWORTH   112
  LONGFELLOW

Full Moon VITA SACKVILLE-WEST   114

The Moon has Set SAPPHO   114

Acquainted with the Night ROBERT FROST   115

Madame Mouse EDITH SITWELL   115

The Song of the Jellicles T. S. ELIOT   116

The Prayer of the Cock CARMEN BERNOS   118
  DE GASZTOLD *translated by Rumer Godden*

Index of First Lines   121

Acknowledgements   124

Cocklight

The first sound that breaks the stillness of the small
hours – those hours between midnight and dawn – is the
crowing of the cock, the first hint of day:

D o not forget, Lord,
it is I who make the sun rise.
I am Your servant
but, with the dignity of my calling,
I need some glitter and ostentation.
Noblesse oblige . . .
All the same,
I am Your servant,
only . . . do not forget, Lord,
I make the sun rise.

"The Prayer of the Cock" CARMEN BERNOS DE GASZTOLD
Translator: Rumer Godden

I 'll tell you how the Sun rose –
A Ribbon at a time –
The Steeples swam in Amethyst –
The news, like Squirrels, ran –
The Hills, untied their Bonnets –
The Bobolinks – begun –
Then I said softly to myself –
"That must have been the Sun"! . . .

"A Day" (extract) EMILY DICKINSON

"Bobolinks" are American singing birds.

E very Thursday morning,
Before you're quite awake,
Without the slightest warning
The house begins to shake
With a Biff! Bang!
Biff! Bang! Bash!

It's the Dustman, who begins
(Bang! Crash!)
To empty both the bins
Of their rubbish and their ash,
With a Biff! Bang!
Biff! Bang! Bash!

"The Dustman" CLIVE SAMSON

All night long while you have been asleep trains have been taking the mail from one city, town or village to another. In this poem, called "Night Mail", the train is really going from London to Glasgow in Scotland, but some of the verses fit any town just as well:

T his is the night mail crossing the border,
Bringing the cheque and the postal order,
Letters for the rich, letters for the poor,
The shop at the corner and the girl next door.
Pulling up Beattock, a steady climb –
The gradient's against her, but she's on time.

Past cotton grass and moorland boulder
Shovelling white steam over her shoulder,

Snorting noisily as she passes
Silent miles of wind-bent grasses.
Birds turn their heads as she approaches,
Stare from the bushes at her blank-faced coaches.
Sheepdogs cannot turn her course,
They slumber on with paws across.
In the farm she passes no one wakes,
But a jug in the bedroom gently shakes.

. . . Letters of thanks, letters from banks,
Letters of joy from girl and boy,
Receipted bills and invitations
To inspect new stock or visit relations,
And applications for situations,
And timid lovers' declarations,
And gossip, gossip from all the nations,
News circumstantial, news financial,
Letters with holiday snaps to enlarge in,
Letters with faces scrawled in the margin.

Letters from uncles, cousins and aunts,
Letters to Scotland from the South of France,
Letters of condolence to Highlands and Lowlands,
Notes from overseas to the Hebrides –
Written on paper of every hue,
The pink, the violet, the white and the blue,
The chatty, the catty, the boring, the adoring,
The cold and official and the heart's outpouring,
Clever, stupid, short and long,
The typed and the printed and the spelt all wrong.

Thousands are still asleep
. . . But shall wake soon and long for letters,
And none will hear the postman's knock
Without a quickening of the heart,
For who can hear and feel himself forgotten?

"Night Mail" (extract) W.H.AUDEN

*When you read that poem aloud you can hear the
rhythm of the train from the slow first verse, gathering
speed after "she's on time" – read more quickly – then
slowing down, bumpitty bumpitty, after "spelt all wrong".*

But some children won't get up:

M innie and Winnie
 Slept in a shell.
Sleep, little ladies!
And they slept well.

Pink was the shell within,
Silver without;
Sounds of the great sea
Wander'd about.

Sleep, little ladies!
Wake not soon!
Echo on echo
Dies to the moon.

Two bright stars
Peep'd into the shell.
"What are they dreaming of?
Who can tell?"

Started a green linnet
Out of the croft;
Wake, little ladies,
The sun is aloft!

"Minnie and Winnie" ALFRED, LORD TENNYSON

A green linnet is a small bird and now all the birds begin their morning chorus. In this poem the rhythm dips and soars and skims like a joyous flying bird:

I cling and swing
On a branch, or sing
Through the cool, clear hush of morning, O!
Or fling my wing
On the air, and bring
To sleepier birds a warning, O!
That the night's in flight,
And the sun's in sight,
And the dew is the grass adorning, O!

And the green leaves swing
As I sing, sing, sing,
Up by the river,
Down the dell,
To the little wee nest,
Where the big tree fell,
So early in the morning, O!

I flit and twit
In the sun for a bit
When his light so bright is shining, O!
Or sit and fit
My plumes, or knit
Straw plaits for the nest's nice lining, O!
And she with glee
Shows unto me
Underneath her wings reclining, O!
And I sing that Peg
Has an egg, egg, egg,
Up by the oat-field,
Round the mill,
Past the meadow,
Down by the hill,
So early in the morning, O!

I stoop and swoop
On the air, or loop
Through the trees, and then go soaring, O!
To group with a troop
On the gusty poop
While the wind behind is roaring, O!
I skim and swim
By a cloud's red rim
And up to the azure flooring, O!

And my wide wings drip
As I slip, slip, slip
Down through the rain-drops,
Back where Peg
Broods in the nest
On the little white egg,
So early in the morning, O!

"The Fifteen Acres" JAMES STEPHENS

Peg is the bird's wife. By "azure flooring" he means the blue sky.

Now you have to wash, dress and brush your hair, but there are some children, chiefly boys, who don't wash at all:

Just look at him! There he stands,
With his nasty hair and hands.
See! his nails are never cut;
They are grim'd as black as soot;
And the sloven, I declare,
Never once has comb'd his hair;
Anything to me is sweeter
Than to see Shock-headed Peter.

"Shock-headed Peter" HEINRICH HOFFMANN

But if you were a fairy's child you wouldn't have to worry about any of these things. You would wash in the dew, the wind would brush your hair:

Children born of fairy stock
Never need for shirt or frock
Never want for food or fire,
Always got their heart's desire:
Jingle pockets full of gold,
Marry when they're seven years old.
Every fairy child may keep
Two strong ponies and ten sheep;
All have houses, each his own,
Built of brick or granite stone;
They live on cherries, they run wild –
I'd love to be a Fairy's child.

"I'd Love to be a Fairy's Child" ROBERT GRAVES

But at last you are ready. The morning waits for you:

The year's at the spring,
And day's at the morn;
Morning's at seven;
The hill-side's dew-pearled;
The lark's on the wing;
The snail's on the thorn:
God's in his heaven –
All's right with the world!

"Pippa Passes" ROBERT BROWNING

Breakfast
and
Out of Doors

Perhaps, like this poet, you have an egg for breakfast:

Thou mak'st my teeming Hen to lay
  Her egg each day:
Besides my healthful Ewes to bear
Me twins each year:
The while the conduits of my Kine
Run Cream (for Wine)
All these, and better Thou does send
Me, to this end,
That I should render for my part
A thankful heart.

"A Thanksgiving to God" ROBERT HERRICK

Kine are cows and ewes are female sheep – what my children called lady sheep!

We have good things to eat and drink, but do you ever wonder where they come from? What about milk?

Half the time they munched the grass,
and all the time they lay
Down in the water-meadows, the lazy month of May,
A-chewing,
A-mooing,
To pass the hours away.

"Nice weather," said the brown cow,
"Ah," said the white.
"Grass is very tasty."
"Grass is all right."

Half the time they munched the grass,
and all the time they lay
Down in the water-meadows, the lazy month of May,
A-chewing,
A-mooing,
To pass the hours away.

"Rain coming," said the brown cow,
"Ah," said the white.
"Flies is very tiresome."
"Flies bite."

Half the time they munched the grass,
and all the time they lay
Down in the water-meadows, the lazy month of May,
A-chewing,
A-mooing,
To pass the hours away.

"Time to go," said the brown cow,
"Ah," said the white.
"Nice chat." "Very pleasant."
"Night." "Night."

"Cows" JAMES REEVES

Most of us like butter. The King liked it very, very much:

The King asked
The Queen, and
The Queen asked
The Dairymaid:
"Could we have some butter for
The Royal slice of bread?"
The Queen asked
The Dairymaid,
The Dairymaid
Said, "Certainly,
I'll go and tell
The cow
Now
Before she goes to bed."

The Dairymaid
She curtsied,
And went and told
The Alderney:
"Don't forget the butter for
The Royal slice of bread."
The Alderney
Said sleepily: "You'd better tell
His Majesty
That many people nowadays
Like marmalade
instead."

The Dairymaid
Said "Fancy!"
And went to
Her Majesty.
She curtsied to the Queen, and
She turned a little red:
"Excuse me,
Your Majesty
For taking of
The liberty,
But marmalade is tasty, if
It's very
Thickly
Spread."

The Queen said
"Oh!"
And went to
His Majesty:
"Talking of the butter for
The Royal slice of bread,
Many people nowadays
Think that
Marmalade
is nicer.
Would you like to try a little
Marmalade
Instead?"

The King said,
"Bother!"
And then he said, "Oh, deary me!"
The King sobbed, "Oh, deary me!"
And went back to bed.
"Nobody,"
He whimpered,
"Could call me
A fussy man;
I only want
A little bit
Of butter for
My bread!"

The Queen said,
"There, there!"
And went to
The Dairymaid.
The Dairymaid
Said, "There, there!"
And went to the shed.
The cow said,
"There, there!
I didn't really
Mean it;
Here's milk for his porringer
And butter for his bread."

The Queen took
The butter
And brought it to
His Majesty;
The King said,
"Butter, eh?"
And bounced out of bed.
"Nobody," he said,
As he kissed her
Tenderly,
"Nobody," he said,
As he slid down
The banisters,
"Nobody,
My darling,
Could call me
A fussy man –

BUT
"I do like a little bit of
butter to my bread!"

"The King's Breakfast" A. A. MILNE

*To eat all these good things you have probably been told
you should have nice table manners, as nice as this
Madam Eglantine, a nun from long ago, though she did
feed her little dogs at the table which nobody should do:*

There also was a Nun, a Prioress;
  Simple her way of smiling was and coy.
Her greatest oath was only "By St Loy!"
And she was known as Madam Eglantine . . .

At meat her manners were well taught withal;
No morsel from her lips did she let fall,
Nor dipped her fingers in the sauce too deep;
But she could carry a morsel up and keep
The smallest drop from falling on her breast.
For courtliness she had a special zest.

And she would wipe her upper lip so clean
That not a trace of grease was to be seen
Upon the cup when she had drunk; to eat,
She reached a hand sedately for the meat.
. . . And she had little dogs she would be feeding
With roasted flesh, or milk, or fine white bread.

"Madam Eglantine" (extract) GEOFFREY CHAUCER

And there are always surprises:

Ann, Ann!
Come! Quick as you can!
There's a fish that talks
In the frying-pan.
Out of the fat,
As clear as glass,
He put up his mouth
And moaned "Alas!"
Oh most mournful,
"Alas, alack!"
Then turned to his sizzling,
And sank him back.

"Alas! Alack!" WALTER DE LA MARE

We cannot stay too long over breakfast; the morning is best out of doors:

All things that love the sun are out of doors;
The sky rejoices in the morning's birth.
The grass is bright with raindrops; on the moors
The hare is running races in her mirth,
And with her feet she from the plashy earth
Raises a mist; that glittering in the sun
Runs with her all the way, wherever she doth run . . .

"Out of Doors" (extract) WILLIAM WORDSWORTH

The rain has silver sandals
For dancing in the spring,
And shoes with golden tassels
For summer's frolicking.
Her winter boots have hobnails
Of ice from heel to toe,
Which now and then she changes
For moccasins of snow.

"The Rain" MAY JUSTUS

On the way to school, suddenly there comes a sound, a loud insistent sound, breaking the morning:

Nine-o'Clock Bell!
Nine-o'Clock Bell!
All the small children and big ones as well,
Pulling their socks up, snatching their hats,
Cheeking and grumbling and giving back-chats,
Laughing and quarrelling, dropping their things,
These at a snail's pace, and those upon wings,
Lagging behind a bit, running ahead,
Waiting at corners for lights to turn red,
Some of them scurrying,
Others not worrying,
Carelessly trudging or anxiously hurrying,
All through the streets they are coming pell-mell
At the Nine-o'Clock
Nine-o'Clock
Nine-o'Clock
Bell!

"Nine-o'Clock Bell" ELEANOR FARJEON

School
Morning

*Though you speak English, the first thing you have to
learn at school is English. How to read and write it.
"Chear" should really be spelt "cheer"; but this poet
could not spell!*

P iping down the valleys wild,
  Piping songs of pleasant glee,
On a cloud I saw a child,
And he laughing said to me:

"Pipe a song about a Lamb!"
So I piped with merry chear.
"Piper, pipe that song again;"
So I piped: he wept to hear.

Drop thy pipe, thy happy pipe;
"Sing thy songs of happy chear:"
So I sung the same again,
While he wept with joy to hear.

"Piper, sit thee down and write
In a book, that all may read."
So he vanished from my sight,
And I pluck'd a hollow reed,

And I made a rural pen,
And I stain'd the water clear,
And I wrote my happy songs
Every child may joy to hear.

"Piping Down the Valleys Wild" WILLIAM BLAKE

Have you ever thought about words, their sound and meaning?

As gardens grow with flowers
English grows with words,
Words that have secret powers,
Words that give joy like birds.

Some of the words you say,
Both in and out of school,
Are brighter than the day,
And deeper than a pool.

Some words there are that dance,
Some words there are that sigh,
The fool's words come by chance,
The poet's to heaven fly.

"Words" (extract) ELEANOR FARJEON

You may be a mathematics person or you may not, but for every child how lovely it would be if the arithmetic bird of this poem suddenly came into the classroom. The bird is a lyre-bird, which has a tail like a beautiful, many-coloured harp; it brought the song of play into the lesson. The teacher could not see it, but the children could; one child hid it in his desk but they all knew about it and listened to its music:

Two and two four
four and four eight
eight and eight sixteen . . .
Once again! says the master
Two and two four
four and four eight
eight and eight sixteen.
But look! the lyre-bird
high on the wing
the child sees it
the child hears it
the child calls it
Save me
play with me
bird!
So the bird alights
and plays with the child
Two and two four . . .
Once again! says the master
and the child plays
and the bird plays too . . .

Four and four eight
eight and eight sixteen
and twice sixteen makes nothing
least of all thirty-two
any-how
and off they go.
For the child has hidden
the bird in his desk
and all the children
hear its song
and all the children
hear the music
and eight and eight in their turn
off they go
and four and four and two and
two
in their turn fade away
and one and one make neither
one nor two
but one by one off they go.
And the lyre-bird sings
and the child sings
and the master shouts
When you've quite finished
playing the fool!
But all the children
are listening to the music
and the walls of the classroom
quietly crumble.

The windowpanes turn
once more to sand
the ink is sea
the desk is trees
the chalk is cliffs
and the quill pen
a bird again.

"Exercise Book" JACQUES PREVERT
  Translator: Paul Dehn

*Some children are shy and don't want anyone to
notice them:*

I'm Nobody! Who are you?
Are you – Nobody – too?
Then there's a pair of us! Don't tell!
They'd banish us – you know!

How dreary – to be – Somebody!
How public – like a Frog –
To tell your name – the livelong day –
To an admiring bog!

"I'm Nobody" EMILY DICKINSON

History is a wonderful lesson; if your teacher can make the men, women and children come alive, it is a succession of stories. One of the most interesting is the story of Abraham Lincoln, a poor boy who by his own efforts rose to be President of the United States of America and one of the greatest of all presidents. He ended slavery – think what it would be like to be sold away from your father and mother, brothers, sisters and everyone you know. In his own words, he made the government "a government of the people, by the people, for the people" which was quite new; they had always been governed by men set far above them.

Children should thank him too because it was he who started Thanksgiving Day, with its turkeys and pumpkin pies. Yet he was a boy who, when he had spent his precious pennies on a book, was too poor to buy a candle to read it by:

There was a boy of other days,
    A quiet, awkward, earnest lad,
Who trudged long weary miles to get
A book on which his heart was set –
And then no candle had!

He was too poor to buy a lamp
But very wise in woodmen's ways.
He gathered seasoned bough and stem,
And crisping leaf, and kindled them
Into a ruddy blaze.

Then as he lay full length and read,
The firelight flickered on his face,
And etched his shadow on the gloom,
And made a picture in the room,
In that most humble place.

The hard years came, the hard years went,
But, gentle, brave, and strong of will,
He met them all. And when today
We see his pictured face, we say,
"There's light upon it still."

"Lincoln" NANCY BYRD TURNER

Perhaps you have a percussion band in your school and
sometimes you play pop or jazz. This is a band which
plays in every mood: happy, sad, noisy, lonesome. The
racing cars don't really out-race the cops; people don't
really fight or tumble down the stairs in a cinch; the
steamboat does not really come hooting up the Mississippi
river, but the music makes you feel they do:

D rum on your drums, batter on your banjos, sob on
your long cool winding saxophones,
Go to it, O jazzmen.
Sling your knuckles on the bottoms of the happy tin pans,
Let your trombones ooze, and go hush-a-hush-a-hush on
the slippery sandpaper.

Moan like an autumn wind high in the lonesome tree-tops,
Moan soft like you wanted somebody terrible,
Cry like a racing car slipping away from a motor-cycle cop,
Bang bang, you jazzmen! Bang all together, drums, traps,
    banjos, horns, tin-cans!
Make two people fight on the top of a stairway and
    scratch each other's eyes in a clinch tumbling down
    the stairs.
Can the rough stuff!
Now a Mississippi steamboat pushes up the night river
    with a hoo-hoo-hoo-oo . . .
And the green lanterns are calling to the high soft stars . . .
And a red moon rides on the humps of the low river
    hills . . .
Go to it, O jazzmen!

"Jazz Fantasia" CARL SANDBERG

I had a little nut-tree,
  nothing would it bear
But a silver nutmeg
    and a golden pear;
The King of Spain's daughter
    came to visit me,
And all for the sake of
    my little nut-tree.
I skipped over water,
    I danced over sea,
And all the birds in the air
    couldn't catch me.

TRADITIONAL

*Towards the end of morning lessons the time begins to
drag; you feel hungry, fidgety and long to be out of
school. One of the best descriptions of children being "let
out" comes from Robert Browning's "Pied Piper of
Hamelin" – that strange piper in his clothes of red and
yellow who, to make the Mayor and Aldermen of
Hamelin pay for their shameful treatment of him, stole
all the children of the town and took them away:*

O nce more he stept into the street:
        And to his lips again
Laid his long pipe of smooth straight cane;
    And ere he blew three notes (such sweet
Soft notes as yet musician's cunning
    Never gave the enraptured air)
There was a rustling, that seemed like a bustling
Of merry crowds jostling at pitching and hustling,
Small feet were pattering, wooden shoes clattering,
Little hands clapping and little tongues chattering,
And, like fowls in a farm-yard when barley is scattering,
Out came the children running.
All the little boys and girls,
With rosy cheeks and flaxen curls,
And sparkling eyes and teeth like pearls,
Tripping and skipping, ran merrily after
The wonderful music with shouting and laughter . . .

"The Pied Piper" (extract) ROBERT BROWNING

Lunch Break

*The first thing – and the most important – when you
break for lunch is food, but no matter what there is or the
dinner lady gives you, the best thing is to go out and buy
a bag of chips:*

Out of the paper bag
Comes the hot breath of the chips
And I shall blow on them
To stop them burning my lips.

Before I leave the counter
The woman shakes
Raindrops of vinegar on them
And salty snowflakes.

Outside the frosty pavements
Are slippery as a slide
But the chips and I
Are warm inside.

"Chips" STANLEY COOK

After you have had your lunch you probably feel more like yourself: warm inside, as the last poet said, and contented, which is what food is for:

It's a very odd thing –
   As odd as can be –
That whatever Miss T. eats
   Turns into Miss T.;
Porridge and apples,
   Mince, muffins and mutton,
Jam, junket, jumbles –
   Not a rap, not a button
It matters; the moment
   They're out of her plate,
Though shared by Miss Butcher
   And sour Mr Bate;
Tiny and Cheerful,
   And neat as can be,
Whatever Miss T. eats
   Turns into Miss T.

"Miss T." WALTER DE LA MARE

You probably go into the playground, perhaps to play.
This is a skipping song; you can hear the rope going
round:

When bread-and-cheese
On hawthorn trees
Makes buds of tiny green;
When big dogs chase
Around and little
Dogs run in between;
When shouts and songs
And arguments
Are heard on every lip
Then is the time
When all true-minded
Children want to skip.

To skip-skip-skip-skip-skip-skip-skip;
It's the time-when-all-the-children-want to skip.

. . . There's skipping ropes
So thin and light
It's hard to twirl them round;
There's hairy ropes
With knots, and heavy
Ropes that slap the ground;
And bits of plastic
Washing-line
Are there among the rest;
But of all the ropes
The rope with painted
Handles is the best.

It's the best-best-best-best-best-best-best;
The rope-with-painted-handles is-the-best –
That's Mine!

"Skipping Song" JOHN WALSH

*Children in the playground with one another always say
what they think, and very plainly if they don't like
someone:*

Tell Tales
Tattle tale, tattle tale,
Hang your britches on a nail.
Tattle tail, tattle tail
Hanging on the bull's tail.

Swankpots
Lily Smith, tall and slender,
She's got legs like a crooked fender.
Long legs, crooked thighs,
Little head and two black eyes.

Nosy Parkers – squashed tomatoes
Mind your own business,
Fry your own fish,
Don't poke your nose
Into my clean dish.

Someone who won't be teased
Roses are red
Violets are blue
Lemons are sour
And so are you.

TRADITIONAL

Children have been singing these rude rhymes for more
than a hundred years, but the playground is also the
place for making friends. Have you ever linked little
fingers with your best friend and said:

Make friends, break friends
We'll never never break friends.

Or, if you've quarrelled:

Break friends, make friends
We'll never make friends.

It can be a friendship between a boy and girl, but that is usually slower – and lasts longer:

Laura's new this year in school.
She acts so opposite, it seems like a rule.
If someone says yes, Laura says no.
If someone says high, Laura says low.
If you say bottom, she'll say top.
If you say go, she'll say stop.
If you say short, Laura says tall.
If you say none, she says all.
If you say beginning, Laura says end . . .
but today she asked me to be her friend.
I said maybe
but not quite yes.
Then I said, "Want to take a walk?"
And Laura said, "I guess."

"Laura" JEFF MOSS

Boys and girls at school can fall in love, mostly in secret, now and again for always – but usually not:

On Monday, Monday,
My True Love said to me,
"I've brought you this nice pumpkin;
I picked it off a tree!"

On Tuesday, Tuesday,
My True Love said to me,
"Look – I've brought you sand tarts;
I got them by the sea."

On Wednesday, Wednesday,
My True Love said to me,
"I've caught you this white polar bear;
It came from Tennessee."

On Thursday, Thursday,
My True Love said to me,
"This singing yellow butterfly
I've all for you, from me."

On Friday, Friday,
My True Love said to me,
"Here's a long-tailed guinea pig;
It's frisky as can be."

On Saturday, Saturday,
to my True Love I said,
"You have not told me ONE TRUE THING,
So you I'll never wed!"

"My True Love" IVY O. EASTWICK

*Maybe, though, you don't want to be with anyone or
do anything but just sit idle, and the playground seems to
melt away:*

U nder the greenwood tree,
  Who loves to lye with me,
And turne his merrie Note
Unto the sweet Bird's throte:
Come hither, come hither, come hither,
    Here shall he see no enemie
But Winter and rough Weather.

Who doth ambition shunne
And loves to live i' the Sunne,
Seeking the food he eates
And pleased with what he gets:
Come hither, come hither, come hither,
    Here shall he see no enemie
But Winter and rough Weather.

"Under the Greenwood Tree" WILLIAM SHAKESPEARE

*"You mustn't daydream," grown-ups say to you, but they
forget that it is when you are still, idle and alone that
thoughts can come to you and turn into poems, stories
and happenings. Or, perhaps, while you are dreaming,
you want to get away from the playground and school,
even from home:*

Do you need a cabin boy,
Ship in the harbour?
Do you need a cabin boy,
Ship on the sea?
I want to go to Africa,
India and China;
So if you're off to foreign parts,
Please take me!

I'm pretty good at polishing,
Ship in the harbour,
And quick at running messages,
Ship on the sea;
It's all right here for ladies,
Little girls and babies;
But if it's cabin boys you want,
Do take me!

I'm tired of the things I know,
Ship in the harbour,
I'm tired of the streets I know,
Ship on the sea;
I don't like shoes with laces,
Collars, ties and braces;
So if you're off to foreign parts
Do take me!

I'm tired of stupid places,
And people's ugly faces,
And if you're off to Round-the-World
Please take me!

"Cabin Boy" CARYL BRAHMS

It is difficult to drag yourself out of a daydream and go back to school. This boy lived in the time of Henry VIII of England and grew up to be the famous Sir Thomas More who dared to oppose the King. In this poem he is only six or seven years old. His rebellious voice rings down five hundred years to us. I am not sure what a cokstele is, perhaps a shuttlecock:

I am called Childhood, in play is all my mind,
To cast a coit, a cokstele, and a ball.
A top can I set, and drive it in his kind,
But would to God these hatefull bookes all,
were in a fire burnt to powder small.
Then might I lead my life always in play:
Which life God send me to mine ending day.

"Childhood" SIR THOMAS MORE

School
Afternoon

*Little Thomas More would have been amazed if he could
have come to your school and, I'm sure, not rebellious.
Though, as you heard, he had a coit, a cokstele and a
ball, and though people played a rough sort of football
then, in those days the last place for games was school.
He probably had to spend hours sitting on a hard stool or
bench and was beaten if he wriggled or yawned. What
would he have said to your being taught, in school hours,
to play cricket and netball, hockey, baseball and football?*

W histle! A kick! A rush, a scramble, a scrum,
   The forwards are busy already, the halves hover
      round,
The three-quarters stand in backwards diverging lines,
Eagerly bent, atoe, with elbows back,
And hands that would grasp at a ball, trembling to start,
While the solid backs vigilant stray about
And the crowd gives out a steady resolute roar,
Like the roar of a sea; a scrum, a whistle, a scrum;
A burst, a whistle, a scrum, a kick into touch;
All in the middle of the field. He is tossing it in,
They have got it and downed it, and hurry, oh, here
   they come . . .
. . . They are scrumming again below . . .
. . . They push, and push and push;
The opponents yield, the fortress wall goes down,
The ram goes through, an irresistible rush
Crosses the last white line, and tumbles down,
And the ball is there. A try! A try! A try! . . .

"The Rugger Match" (extract) SIR JOHN SQUIRE

Nor did children in Thomas More's time do things in school like carpentry, modelling or sewing. A sewing basket can be a precious possession, and this poet has made a nonsense poem about the things you keep in it; it is a clever poem because the words are as spiky and prickly and jumbled as anything in the basket:

Needles and ribbons and packets of pins,
Prints and chintz and odd bod-a-kins,
They's never mind whether
You laid 'em together
Or one from the other in pockets and tins.

For packets of pins and ribbons and needles
Or odd bod-a-kins, and chintz and prints,
Being birds of a feather,
Would huddle together
Like minnows on billows or pennies in mints.

"Pincushion Song" ROBERT GRAVES

There is great satisfaction, even joy, in making things by
hand, especially now, when so many things are made by
machine in hundreds and thousands. What you make
yourself is only one, unique – there will never be another
exactly like it – and, always, a little of yourself
goes into it:

Things men have made with wakened hands, and put
  soft life into
are awake through years with transferred touch, and go on
    glowing
for long years.
And for this reason, some old things are lovely
warm still with the life of forgotten men who made them.

Whatever man makes and makes it live
lives because of the life put into it.
A yard of India muslin is alive with Hindu life.
And a Navajo woman, weaving her rug in the pattern of
    her dream,
must run the pattern out in a little break at the end
so that her soul can come out, back to her.

But in the odd pattern, like snake-marks on the sand,
it leaves its trail.

"Things Men Have Made" D. H. LAWRENCE

But sometimes it is not as easy; in drawing and painting it often seems impossible to catch what you see or imagine and put it on paper, as in this poem, "How to Paint the Portrait of a Bird":

First paint a cage
with an open door
then paint
something pretty
something simple
something fine
something useful
for the bird
next place the canvas against a tree
in a garden
in a wood
or in a forest
hide behind the tree
without speaking
without moving . . .
Sometimes the bird comes quickly
but it can also take many years
before making up its mind
Don't be discouraged
wait
wait if necessary for years
the quickness or the slowness of the coming
of the bird having no relation
to the success of the picture.

When the bird comes
if it comes
observe the deepest silence
wait for the bird to enter the cage
and when it has entered
gently close the door with the paint-brush
then
one by one paint out all the bars
taking care not to touch one feather of the bird
Next make a portrait of the tree
choosing the finest of its branches
for the bird
paint also the green leaves and the freshness of the wind
dust in the sun
and the sound of the insects in the summer grass
and wait for the bird to decide to sing.
If the bird does not sing
it is a bad sign
a sign that the picture is bad
but if it sings it is a good sign
a sign that you are ready to sign
so then you pluck very gently
one of the quills of the bird
and you write your name in the corner of the picture.

"How to Paint the Portrait of a Bird" JACQUES PREVERT
Translator: Paul Dehn

*No school is complete without computers. I couldn't find
a poem about them so I asked the boys and girls at a
school nearby to write some for me. Here is one of
the best:*

Now I'm really, really extremely tired,
For the NEXT time I'll use my BBC,
Will be many, many years from now,
You REPEAT UNTIL it understands,
I think it's known as an INTERFACE problem,
I almost believe computers BYTE!

One day I'll BREAK this thing,
Into tiny little BITS,
I think it eats MICROCHIPS
(With very large GOBYTES!)
All these errors it gives,
It really MEGAHERTZ me!

There'll be streams of TAPE-STREAMER,
Showers of CARTRIDGES and MICROCOMPUTER,
Doing CIRCUITS in the ceiling,
Closely followed by PCBs and LOGO,
MINICOMPUTERS and MAINFRAMES,
Knocking MEGABYTES and KILOBYTES off the wall!

My mother came in and emitted a scream
(Her nerves are in VOLATILE MEMORY).
She ran to the first aid box for a GRAPHICS TABLET,
I crawled to the powerswitch and shut it down,
It was such a great pity to stop all this,
It was such a SUPERCOMPUTER I had!

"Computer" JAMES SUTHERLAND, aged 11

I have always thought geography was the best lesson;
the very soil your school stands on, gardens and parks,
countries and continents, rice fields and ice fields, camels,
elephants and flying ants are all geography, as are
mountains, rivers and towns with curious names:

When I was but thirteen or so
I went into a golden land
Chimborazo, Cotopaxi
Took me by the hand.

My father died, my brother too,
They passed like fleeting dreams,
I stood where Popocatepetl
In the sunlight gleams.

I dimly heard the master's voice
And boys far-off at play,
Chimborazo, Cotopaxi
had stolen me away.

I walked in a great golden dream
To and fro from school –
Shining Popocatepetl
The dusty streets did rule.

I walked home with a gold dark boy
And never a word I'd say,
Chimborazo, Cotopaxi
Had taken my speech away:

I gazed entranced upon his face
Fairer than any flower –
O shining Popocatepetl
It was thy magic hour:

The houses, people, traffic seemed
Thin fading dreams by day,
Chimborazo, Cotopaxi
They had stolen my soul away!

"Romance" W. J. TURNER

"Popocatepetl" is a volcano in Mexico.

Geography is the beginning of adventure; today you can easily go by aeroplane to most of those far-off places, but much the best adventuring is to go by sea. In 1947 six adventurers, under a Norwegian captain, crossed the Pacific on a raft made of nine logs of balsa wood lashed side by side, pointed with splashboards at the prow. Its mast bore a four-pointed sail painted with a bearded face – because this raft was the famous Kon-Tiki *and Kon-Tiki means 'son of the Sun'. There was a cane-work cabin which was home, for a hundred days, for six men, a parrot ...*

'and a small tame crab
Whose name was Johnny; he lived in a hole
   near the steering block
And came when he was called.'

The poet gives a wonderful sea-picture of their days and nights:

They were not lonely. They found the sea
  No barren waste but a living world,
Peopled as the woodland with wild creatures,
Curious and shy. The rough-riding steamer
With his foaming prow and his engine roar
Sees them not. But Kon-Tiki scared them not away.
As timid birds at twilight hop and twitter
On the summer lawn about the quiet house,
So now about the noiseless floating raft

The frolicking sea-dwellers. Then did Ocean,
The great showman, out of the bountiful deep
Conjure all manner of strange creatures
To delight them: flying fish that shot through the air
Like quicksilver, smack against the sail,
Then dropped to deck into the breakfast saucepan
Waiting there; the prosperous tunny,
Fat as an alderman with rows of double chins;
The glorious dolphin, bluebottle-green
With glittering golden fins, greedy
For the succulent weed that trailed like garlands
From the steering oar. There were many more . . .
These marvels were the day's. What words
Can paint the night,
When the sea was no darkness but a universe of light?
Lo, in their wake a shoal
Of little shrimps, all shining,
A sprinkle of red coal!

Drawn by the gleaming cabin lamp, the octopus,
The giant squid with green ghostly eyes,
Hugged and hypnotized;
While, fathoms below, in the pitch-black deep were gliding
Balloons of flashing fire, silver
Streaming meteors. O world of wonder!
O splendid pageantry!
Hour after dreamy hour they gazed spell-bound,
Trailing their fingers in the starry sea.

"The Ballad of the Kon-Tiki" (extract) IAN SERRAILLIER

*If you go to other countries, even if it is only visiting
and not adventuring, it is a great help to speak their
languages. Perhaps you are already beginning with one
– French. Things sound quite different in French, as you
can hear in this translation of a poem that many of you
will know: "The Owl and the Pussycat" becomes "Le
Hibou et la Poussiquette":*

Hibou et Minou allèrent à la mer
Dans une barque peinte en jaune-canari;
Ils prirent du miel roux et beaucoup de sous
Enroulés dans une lettre de crédit.
Le hibou contemplait les astres du ciel,
Et chantait, en grattant sa guitare
"O Minou chérie, O Minou ma belle,
O Poussiquette, comme tu es rare,
Es rare,
Es rare!
O Poussiquette, comme tu es rare!"

Try saying the Owl's song aloud in French and you will hear how enchanting it sounds. Here is the poem in English:

The Owl and the Pussy-Cat went to sea
In a beautiful pea-green boat:
They took some honey, and plenty of money
Wrapped up in a five-pound note.
The Owl looked up to the stars above,
And sang to a small guitar,
"O lovely Pussy, O Pussy, my love,
What a beautiful Pussy you are,
You are,
You are!
What a beautiful Pussy you are!"

Pussy said to the Owl, "You elegant fowl!
How charmingly sweet you sing!
O let us be married! too long we have tarried:
But what shall we do for a ring?"
They sailed away for a year and a day,
To the land where the Bong-tree grows,
And there in a wood a Piggy-wig stood,
With a ring at the end of his nose,
His nose,
His nose,
With a ring at the end of his nose.

"Dear Pig, are you willing to sell for one shilling
Your ring?" Said the Piggy, "I will."
So they took it away, and were married next day
By the Turkey who lives on the hill.
They dined on mince, and slices of quince,
Which they ate with a runcible spoon;
And hand in hand, on the edge of the sand,
They danced by the light of the moon,
The moon,
The moon,
They danced by the light of the moon – *au clair de la lune.*

"The Owl and the Pussycat" EDWARD LEAR
Translator: Frances Steegmuller

It comes as quite a shock to hear the bell. In a few minutes school will be out:

Girls scream,
Boys shout;
Dogs bark,
    School's out.

Cats run,
    Horses shy;
Into trees
    Birds fly.

Babes wake
    Open-eyed.
If they can,
    Tramps hide.

Old man,
    Hobble home;
Merry mites,
    Welcome.

"School's Out" W. H. DAVIES

Playtime

*There are fashions in play and you children seem to
catch them from one another without being told: suddenly
you are all doing one thing, next day another, without
a word; it is like the tom-tom drums used to send
messages:*

This is the day for bicycles.
    Yesterday was a swimming day,
        A day for splashing head over heels,
When every child would have screamed dismay
At anything less than dolphin play.
        But today they are all on wheels.
Large and little and middle-sized,
An army of children goes mechanized.
As if for a silver medal,
Around and around they pedal . . .

Tomorrow, or the day after,
    The pedals will lose their power.
Solemn, and yet with laughter,
They will turn to something dafter,
    All at the selfsame hour.
All of a sudden the windy heights
Will burst into gaudy bloom of kites
With a heaven-aspiring reach
And a child attached to each . . .

If you ask them, they are perplext.
　　The calendar gives no warning.
One does not tell the next,
　　Yet they wake and know in the morning
(As a swallow knows the time
　　For quitting a rainy land),
When the rope should whirl to the skipping-rhyme
　　Or the baseball thud in the hand,
Or the multitudinous din
Of the roller skates begin.

It is something that tom-toms say.
You cannot explain it away,
　　Though reason or judgment reels.
For yesterday was a swimming day
And today is the same as yesterday,
　　Yet now they are all on wheels.

"Tom-Tom" (extract) PHYLLIS McGINLEY

I have always wondered what happens to a broken-off kite. Who finds it? Where does it go? This one flew so high it blotted out a star:

Alone, and stirring lightly in the night,
what is there quite as quiet as a broken kite?

What silence is so silent as its whisper
in the highness of its fall? It roosts among
the branches, blotting out a star; it bears
the rains and mornings, every dawn
till it is gone –

It is May; the hem of evening rustles as she
walks beside the pond, the songs of peepers
whispering like circlets at her ankles
clashing
tiny gongs and bells; the stars
dance in the water –
all but one.

"One Star Less" RUSSELL HOBAN

Some games never change, like "catch", or "it":

You can't catch me!
You can't catch me!
Run as swift as quicksilver,
You can't catch me!

If you can catch me you shall have a ball
That once the daughter of a king let fall;
It ran down the hill and it rolled on the plain,
And the king's daughter never caught her ball again.

> And you can't catch me!
> You can't catch me!
> Run as quick as lightning,
> But you can't catch me!

If you can catch me you shall have a bird
That once the son of a beggar heard.
He climbed up the tree, but the bird flew away,
And the beggar's son never caught a bird that day.

> You can't catch me!
> You can't catch me!
> Run as swift as quicksilver.
> You can't catch me!

"Catch" ELEANOR FARJEON

Do you ever play cowboy outlaws? What you miss if you don't! Jesse James was the most famous of them all:

Jesse James was a two-gun man,
  (Roll on Missouri!)
Strong-arm chief of an outlaw clan
(From Kansas to Illinois!)
He twirled an old Colt forty-five
(Roll on, Missouri!)
They never took Jesse James alive.
(Roll, Missouri, roll!)

. . .

Jesse rode through a sleepin' town;
Looked the moonlit street both up an' down;
Crack-crack-crack, the street ran flames
An' a great voice cried, "I'm Jesse James!"

Hawse and foot they're after Jess!
(Roll on, Missouri!)
Spurrin' and spurrin' but he's gone Wes'.
(Brown Missouri rolls!)
He was ten foot tall when he stood in his boots;
(Lightnin' like the Missouri!)
More'n a match for sich galoots.
(Roll, Missouri, roll!)

. . .

They sought him here an' they sought him there,
(Roll on, Missouri!)
But he strides by night through the ways of the air;
(Brown Missouri rolls!)
They say he was took an' they say he was dead,
(Cataracts on the Missouri!)
But he ain't, he's a sunset overhead! –
(Missouri down to the sea!)

. . .

Jesse James wore a red bandanner
That waved on the breeze like the Star-spangled Banner.
In seven States he cut up dadoes.
He's gone with the buffer an' the desperadoes.

Yes, Jesse James was a two-gun man
(Roll on, Missouri!)
The same as when this song began;
(From Kansas to Illinois!)
An' when you see a sunset burst into flames
(Lightnin' like the Missouri!)
Or a thunderstorm blaze – that's Jesse James!
(Hear that Missouri roll!)

"Jesse James" (extracts) WILLIAM ROSE BENET

A Colt is a revolver; the buffer are buffaloes; galoots are awkward, clumsy fellows; dadoes are the bases for statues.

Perhaps you are one of the lucky ones who has a pony and goes riding.

This is a poem about a foal who had been left out in the field when it was getting dark and snowing. A Morgan is a breed of pony:

Once when the snow of the year was beginning to fall,
We stopped by a mountain pasture to say, "Whose
    colt?"
A little Morgan had one forefoot on the wall,
The other curled at his breast. He dipped his head
And snorted at us. And then he had to bolt.
We heard the miniature thunder where he fled,
And we saw him, or thought we saw him, dim and grey,
Like a shadow against the curtain of falling flakes.
"I think the little fellow's afraid of the snow.
He isn't winter-broken. It isn't play
With the little fellow at all. He's running away.
I doubt if even his mother would tell him, 'Sakes,
It's only weather.' He'd think she didn't know!"
"Where is his mother? He can't be out alone."
And now he comes again with a clatter of stone,
And mounts the wall again with whited eyes
And all his tail that isn't hair up straight.
He shudders his coat as if to throw off flies.
"Whoever it is that leaves him out so late,
When other creatures have gone to stall and bin,
Ought to be told to come and take him in."

"The Runaway" ROBERT FROST

Perhaps you like doing things alone, like fishing:

I am cold and alone,
On my tree-root sitting as still as stone.
The fish come to my net. I scorned the sun,
The voices on the road, and they have gone.
My eyes are buried in the cold pond, under
The cold, spread leaves; my thoughts are silver-wet.
I have ten stickleback, a half-day's plunder,
Safe in my jar. I shall have ten more yet.

"A Boy Fishing" E. SCOVELL

*. . . or playing quietly with your dolls' house – American
children say doll house not dolls' house. In this poem the
poet finds her children's old dolls' house put away in the
attic – they are grown up now – and brings it down to
make it live again.*

*Time, dust and mice had not harmed it. "It was
all there, Perfect and little and inviolate", which means
nothing was hurt or broken, except the rocking-chair.
Most people would have to go to the jeweller's to mend
dolls'-house things, but the poet must have had that
touch because soon everything was in order again and
the magic had come back. There is a sort of magic in
miniature things:*

After the children left it, after it stood
For a while in the attic,
Along with the badminton set, and the skis too good
To be given away, and the peerless Automatic
Popcorn Machine that used to fly into rages,
And the Dr. Dolittle books, and the hamsters' cages,
She brought it down once more
To a bedroom, empty now, on the second floor
And put the furniture in.
      There was nothing much
That couldn't be used again with a bit of repair.
It was all there,
Perfect and little and inviolate.
So, with the delicate touch
A jeweller learns, she mended the rocking chair,
Meticulously laundered
The gossamer parlor curtains, dusted the grate,

Glued the glazed turkey to the flowered plate,
And polished the Lilliput writing desk.
    She squandered
One bold October day and half the night
Binding the carpets round with a ribbon border;
Till, to her grave delight
(With the kettle upon the stove, the mirror's face
Scoured the formal sofa set in its place),
She saw the dwelling decorous
And in order . . .
    There stood the dinner table
Invincibly agleam
With the undisheveled candles, the flowers that bloomed
Forever and forever,
The wine that never
Spilled on the cloth or sickened or was consumed.

The Times lay at the doorsill, but it told
Daily the same unstirring report. The fire
Painted upon the hearth would not turn cold,
Or the constant hour change, or the heart tire
Of what it must pursue,
Or the guest depart, or anything here be old.

"The Doll House" (extract) PHYLLIS McGINLEY

It is time for everyone and everything to go inside:

Allie, call the birds in,
The birds from the sky!
Allie calls, Allie sings,
        Down they all fly:
First there come
Two white doves,
        Then a sparrow from his nest
Then a clucking bantam hen
        Then a robin red-breast.

Allie, call the beasts in,
        The beasts, every one!
Allie calls, Allie sings,
        In they all run:
First there came
Two black lambs,
        Then a grunting Berkshire sow,
Then a dog without a tail,
        Then a red and white cow.

Allie, call the fish up,
        The fish from the stream!
Allie calls, Allie sings,
        Up they all swim:
First there came
Two gold fish,
        A minnow and a miller's thumb,
Then a school of little trout,
        Then the twisting eels come.

Allie, call the children,
    Call them from the green!
Allie calls, Allie sings,
    Soon they run in:
First there came
Tom and Madge,
    Kate and I who'll not forget
How we played by the water's edge
    Till the April sun set.

"Allie" ROBERT GRAVES

Teatime, Suppertime and Pets

Most British children have a late tea, American children
an early supper; but just imagine what it would be like to
have a tea party in a spaceship where nothing will stay
down because everything is weightless: the tablecloth lies
by itself in the air; the tea will not stay in the pot but goes
hurtling about in a "wet and steaming ball". The guests
try to hold their cups up but cannot because their hands
are weightless too, while the tea dances in and out of the
cups as if it played cup and ball; in fact the guests never
spill a drop because they never get one. They, poor things,
open their mouths wide to try to catch the flying cakes
and the spinning tarts, while the sugar lumps jet up and
down like a fountain.

This poem is full of difficult words: those of you who
are interested in science will understand them, but those
who do not should not worry; after all, in a spaceship
there are many strange dials and knobs and buttons of
which few of us would know the meaning, so it is fitting
that the poem should be like that; just let a picture of
the party come into your mind:

In this world a tablecloth need not be laid
On any table, but is spread out anywhere
Upon the always equidistant and
Invisible legs of gravity's wild air.

The tea, which never would grow cold,
Gathers itself into a wet and steaming ball,
And hurls its liquid molecules at anybody's head,
Or dances, eternal bilboquet,
In and out of the suspended cups up-
ended in the weightless hands
Of chronically nervous jerks
Who yet would never spill a drop,
Their mouths agape for passing cakes.

Lumps of sparkling sugar
Sling themselves out of their crystal bowl
With a disordered fountain's
Ornamental stops and starts.
The milk describes a permanent parabola
Girdled with satellites of spinning tarts.

The future lives with graciousness.
The hostess finds her problems eased,
For there is honey still for tea
And butter keeps the ceiling greased.

She will provide, of course,
No cake-forks, spoons or knives.
They are so sharp, so dangerously gadabout,
It is regarded as a social misdemeanour
To put them out.

"Tea in a Space Ship" JAMES KIRKUP

A "bilboquet" is two sticks joined together by a cord and used for playing cup and ball. A "parabola" is a curve or curves which can run for ever.

Do you sometimes have soup for supper?

Beautiful Soup, so rich and green,
Waiting in a hot tureen!
Who for such dainties would not stoop?
Soup of the evening, beautiful Soup!
Soup of the evening, beautiful Soup!
  Beau-ootiful Soo-oop!
  Beau-ootiful Soo-oop!
Soo-oop of the e-e-evening,
  Beautiful, beautiful Soup!

Beautiful Soup! Who cares for fish,
Game, or any other dish?
Who would not give all else for two p–
ennyworth only of beautiful Soup?
Pennyworth only of beautiful Soup?
  Beautiful Soup!
  Beautiful Soup!
Soo-oop of the e-e-evening,
  Beau-ti-ful, beauti-FUL SOUP!

"Beautiful Soup" LEWIS CARROLL

This poet sent "a pipkin of jelly" to a lady. It must have been a very little jelly. A "cruse" can be a drinking cup or a bottle:

A little Saint best fits a little Shrine,
A little Prop best fits a little Vine,
As my small Cruse best fits my little Wine.

A little Seed best fits a little Soil,
A little Trade best fits a little Toil:
As my small Jar best fits my little Oil.

A little Bin best fits a little Bread,
A little Garland fits a little Head:
As my small stuff best fits my little Shed.

A little Hearth best fits a little Fire,
A little Chapel fits a little Quire,
As my small Bell best fits my little Spire.

A little stream best fits a little Boat;
A little lead best fits a little Float;
As my small Pipe best fits my little note.

A little meat best fits a little belly,
As sweetly Lady, give me leave to tell ye,
This little Pipkin fits this little Jelly.

"A Ternarie of Littles" ROBERT HERRICK

This little cat is hungry too; her mistress has left her all alone:

It will not do, I must go in
And change my shoes and wash my hands.
Upon the threshold – O my sin –
    Did I forget her? There she stands
With tail upraised and blazing eyes
    And arching back, and many cries.

She had been alone since two
    O'clock had struck – my little cat,
My cuckoo, O my Cockatoo,
    My small, my sweet, my fine, my fat,
My darling, O my first delight,
    My wanton, wishful, fishful sprite.

Then quickly to the larder she,
    And I as she, together fly;
Upon the jug of cream do we
    Together, with a great outcry,
Precipitate ourselves, and on
    The plate of cod as white as snow.

And while I drink my early cup
    Of china tea, she tears her fish;
And whilst I wash my tea things up
    She rattles at her empty dish:
And O, how joyously the clock
    Ticks off the minutes as the flock.

"Everyone has Gone to Town" (extract) FREDEGOND SHOVE

It is odd: there are hundreds of poems about cats but only perhaps a dozen about dogs. Of these few, this one is the most famous. It is told by the dog himself, not strictly in poetry but near-poetry prose. He was a Highland Terrier or Scottie called Boots:

There is walk-in-Park-on-lead. There is off-lead-when-we-come-to-the-grass. There is 'nother dog, like me, off-lead. I say: "Name?" He says: "Slippers." He says: "Name?" I say: "Boots." He says: "I am fine dog. I have Own God called Miss." I say: "I am very fine dog. I have Own God called Master." There is walk-round-on-toes. There is Scrap. There is Proper Whacking. Master says: "Sorry! Awfully sorry! All my fault." Slippers's Miss says: "Sorry! My fault too." Master says: "So glad it is both our faults. Nice little dog, Slippers." Slippers's Miss says: "Do you really think so?" Then I make "Beseech". Slippers's Miss says: "Darling little dog, Boots."
There is on-lead again, and walking with Slippers behind both Own Gods, long times . . . Slippers is not-half-bad dog. Very like me. "Make-fine-pair," Master says . . .

"Thy Servant a Dog" RUDYARD KIPLING

"Own God" is the dogs' name for their owners.

*The most valiant and touching story of a dog's
faithfulness comes from a ballad called "Beth Gêlert".
Gêlert was a great hound given to the Welsh Knight
Llewelyn by King John in the twelfth century. No other
dog could match Gêlert in hunting, but one day he did
not join the hunt:*

Twas only at Llewelyn's board
    The faithful Gêlert fed;
He watched, he served, he cheered his lord,
    And sentinelled his bed.

In sooth he was a peerless hound
    The gift of royal John;
But now no Gêlert could be found
    And all the chase rode on . . .

That day Llewelyn little loved
    The chase of hart and hare;
And scant and small the booty proved,
    For Gêlert was not there.

Unpleased, Llewelyn homeward hied,
    When, near the portal seat,
His truant Gêlert he espied,
    Bounding his lord to greet.

But when he gained his castle door,
    Aghast the chieftain stood;
The hound all o'er was smeared with gore;
    His lips, his fangs, ran blood . . .

O'erturned his infant's bed he found,
    With blood-stained covert rent;
And all around, the walls and ground
    With recent blood bespent.

He called his child – no voice replied –
    He searched with terror wild;
Blood, blood he found on every side,
    But nowhere found his child.

Onward, in haste, Llewelyn passed,
    And on went Gêlert too;
And still where'er his eyes he cast,
    Fresh blood-gouts shocked his view.

"Hell-hound! my child's by thee devoured,"
    The frantic father cried;
And to the hilt his vengeful sword
    He plunged in Gêlert's side.

His suppliant looks, as prone he fell,
    No pity could impart;
But still his Gêlert's dying yell
    Passed heavy o'er his heart.

Aroused by Gêlert's dying yell,
    Some slumberer wakened nigh:
What words the parent's joy could tell
    To hear his infant's cry!

Concealed beneath a tumbled heap
    His hurried search had missed,
All flowing from his rosy sleep,
    The cherub boy he kissed.

Nor scathe had he, nor harm, nor dread,
    But, the same couch beneath,
Lay a gaunt wolf, all torn and dead,
    Tremendous still in death.

Ah, what was then Llewelyn's pain!
    For now the truth was clear;
His gallant hound the wolf had slain
    To save Llewelyn's heir.

Vain, vain was all Llewelyn's woe;
    "Best of thy kind, adieu!
The frantic blow which laid thee low
    This heart shall ever rue" . . .

"Beth Gêlert" (extract) WILLIAM ROBERT SPENCER

*A great many people, grown-ups as well as children, on
reading the last poem, would say, "What a horrid poem",
and never read it again. But didn't it stir you and make
you feel? Poetry is meant to touch us, often deeply,
make us feel that wonderful thing "compassion", which
means sharing with someone, man or dog, in their
suffering; and how often have we said or done something
in our hastiness for which, afterwards, we are bitterly
sorry, like Llewelyn?*

*Not all children can have a dog or a cat, so many of
them have guinea pigs instead, but not, I hope, with
the same results as this – yet the two only had four little
pigs each:*

We had two little guinea pigs
　　They did what guinea pigs
Have always done before
And there were four more.
　　2 x 4 = 8 + the original 2 = 10.

We had ten little guinea pigs
And they did what guinea pigs have
always done
And there were forty
assorti.
　　10 x 4 = 40 + the original 10 = 50. (all colours)

We had fifty little guinea pigs
And they did what guinea pigs have always done
How can they go on and on? I wondered
And we had two hundred.
        50 x 4 = 200 + the original 50 = 250.

Two hundred and fifty little guinea pigs
Did what they have always done
Eating us out of house and home and
There were a thousand.
        250 x 4 = 1000 + the original 250 = 1,250.

Guinea pigs in their fluff and fur are most attractive
But I wish they were not so active
In doing what they have done before –
I can't count any more!

"Guinea Pigs" RUMER GODDEN

Of course, there wouldn't have been so many, as some would have been males, but for the sake of the poem the poet has taken what is called "poetic licence".

But it is getting on towards evening and maybe you and your pets are getting tired:

The shadows flickering, the daylight dying.
   And I upon the old red sofa lying,
The great brown shadows leaping up the wall,
The sparrows twittering; and that is all.

I thought to send my soul to far-off lands,
Where fairies scamper on the windy sands,
Or where the autumn rain comes drumming down
On huddled roofs, in an enchanted town.

But O my sleepy soul, it will not roam,
It is too happy and too warm at home:
With just the shadows leaping up the wall,
The sparrows twittering; and that is all.

"Autumn Evening" FRANCES CORNFORD

Twilight
and Stories
out of
This World

"Twilight" means in-between light, that time in the evening between daylight and darkness when the light turns to dusk:

Sunlight, moonlight,
Twilight, starlight –
Gloaming at the close of day,
And an owl calling,
Cool dews falling
In a wood of oak and may.

Lantern-light, taper-light,
Torchlight, no-light:
Darkness at the shut of day,
And lions roaring,
Their wrath pouring
In wild waste places far away.

Elf-light, bat-light,
Touchwood-light and toad-light,
And the sea a shimmering gloom of grey,
And a small face smiling
In a dream's beguiling
In a world of wonders far away.

"Dream Song" WALTER DE LA MARE

*This time of day is good for stories – probably you
watch them on television – but stories read or told
have a life of their own and the odd part is that you
remember them, which you seldom do with television:*

Little Orphant Annie came to our house to stay,
An' wash the cups an' saucers up and put the things
    away,
An' shoo' the chickens off the porch, an' dust the hearth
    an' sweep,
An' make the fire and bake the bread, an' earn her board
    an' keep.
An' all us other childen when the supper things is done,
We set around the kitchen fire and has the mostest fun,
A-listenin' to the witch tales that Annie tells about,
An' the gobble-uns 'at gits you ef you don't watch out! . . .

An' little Orphant Annie says when the blaze is blue,
An' the lamp wick splutters, an' the wind goes woo-oo!
An' you hear the crickets quit an' the moon is grey,
An' the lightnin' bugs in dew is all squenched away,
You'd better mind your parents an' your teachers fond an'
    dear,
An' cherish them 'at loves you an' dry the orphant's tear,
An' help the poor an' needy ones as clusters all about,
Er the gobble-uns 'll git you ef you don't watch out!

"Little Orphant Annie" JAMES WHITCOMB RILEY

*Americans sometimes say "orphant" instead of
"orphan".*

Witches and giants scare most people, but not Isabel:

Isabel met an enormous bear;
Isabel, Isabel, didn't care.
The bear was hungry, the bear was ravenous,
The bear's big mouth was cruel and cavernous.
The bear said, Isabel, glad to meet you,
How do, Isabel, now I'll eat you!
Isabel, Isabel, didn't worry,
Isabel didn't scream or scurry.
She washed her hands and she straightened her hair up,
Then Isabel quietly ate the bear up.

Once on a night as black as pitch
Isabel met a wicked old witch.
The witch's face was cross and wrinkled,
The witch's gums with teeth were sprinkled.
Ho, ho, Isabel! the old witch crowed,
I'll turn you into an ugly toad!
Isabel, Isabel, didn't worry,
Isabel didn't scream or scurry.
She showed no rage and she showed no rancour,
But she turned the witch into milk and drank her.

Isabel met a hideous giant,
Isabel continued self-reliant.
The giant was hairy, the giant was horrid,
He had one eye in the middle of his forehead.
Good morning, Isabel, the giant said,
I'll grind your bones to make my bread.
Isabel, Isabel, didn't worry,
Isabel didn't scream or scurry.
She nibbled the zwieback that she always fed off,
And when it was gone, she cut the giant's head off.

Isabel met a troublesome doctor,
He punched and he poked till he really shocked her.
The doctor's talk was of coughs and chills
And the doctor's satchel bulged with pills.
The doctor said unto Isabel,
Swallow this, it will make you well.
Isabel, Isabel didn't worry,
Isabel didn't scream or scurry.
She took those pills from the pill-concocter,
And Isabel calmly cured the doctor.

"Adventures of Isabel" OGDEN NASH

"Zwieback" is a kind of crispbread.

*Orphan Annie's "gobble-uns" were goblins. I always
feel sorry for this goblin, who wanted the beads not
for greed but because he loved them:*

Nymph, nymph, what are your beads?
Green glass, goblin. Why do you stare at them?
Give them me.
         No.
Give them me. Give them me.

              No.

Then I will howl all night in the reeds,
Lie in the mud and howl for them.

Goblin, why do you love them so?

They are better than stars or water,
Better than voices of winds that sing,
Better than any man's fair daughter,
Your green glass beads on a silver ring.

Hush, I stole them out of the moon.

Give me your beads, I want them.

              No.

I will howl in a deep lagoon
For your green glass beads, I love them so.
Give them me. Give them me.

              No.

"Overheard on a Saltmarsh" HAROLD MUNRO

A story poem about running away:

Three gypsies stood at the Castle gate,
 They sang so high, they sang so low,
The lady sate in her chamber late,
  Her heart it melted away as snow.

They sang so sweet, they sang so shrill,
  That fast her tears began to flow.
And she laid down her silken gown,
  Her golden rings and all her show.

She plucked off her high-heeled shoes,
  A-made of Spanish leather, O!
She walked in the street, with her bare, bare feet,
  All out in the wind and weather, O!

It was late last night, when my lord came home,
  Enquiring for his a-lady, O!
The servants said on every hand,
  "She's gone with the wraggle taggle gypsies, O!"

"O saddle to me my milk-white steed.
  Go and fetch me my pony, O!
That I may ride and seek my bride,
  Who is gone with the wraggle taggle gypsies, O!"

O he rode high and he rode low,
  He rode through woods and copses too.
Until he came to an open field,
  And there he espied his a-lady, O!

"What makes you leave your house and land?
  What makes you leave your money, O?
What makes you leave your new-wedded lord?
  To go with the wraggle taggle gypsies, O!"

"What care I for my house and my land?
  What care I for my money, O?
What care I for my new-wedded lord?
  I'm off with the wraggle taggle gypsies, O!"

"Last night you slept on a goose-feather bed,
  With the sheet turned down so bravely, O!
And tonight you'll sleep in a cold open field,
  Along with the wraggle taggle gypsies, O!"

"What care I for a goose-feather bed,
  With the sheet turned down so bravely, O?
For tonight I shall sleep in a cold open field,
  Along with the wraggle taggle gypsies, O!"

"The Wraggle Taggle Gypsies" UNKNOWN

*The next is a fabulous poem not only in the sense of
incredible and astonishing – Solomon was the famous
and wise King in the Bible and the Queen of Sheba came
from far away – but fabulous because it has a fabled
animal which no one has ever seen:*

But the Queen of Sheba went with Solomon
To his country house at Lebanon,
Where she brought him gifts of hot-house grapes,
Of ivory,
      of ebony,
           of elephants and apes,
Of peacocks, of pearls, and a hundred pygmy slaves
with skins like an orange, and hair that waves,
and each of them wore a turban,
picked out with the plumes of a pelican:
But of all her gifts, by far the rarest,
Brought from the terrible central forest,
with a vein of gold in its ivory horn,
was a lovelorn milk-white unicorn.

"The Queen of Sheba's Gifts" OSBERT SITWELL

Another fabled animal, even more beautiful than a unicorn, was Pegasus, the white horse with wings whom only a poet could ride. Here, he has strayed into a village; a "pound" is an enclosure with bars where strays and cattle, and sometimes horses, were put for sale:

O nce into a quiet village,
    Without haste and without heed,
In the golden prime of morning,
    Strayed the poet's winged steed.

It was Autumn, and incessant
    Piped the quails from shocks and sheaves,
And, like living coals, the apples
    Burned among the withering leaves . . .

Thus, upon the village common,
    By the schoolboys he was found;
And the wise men, in their wisdom,
    Put him straightway into pound.

Then the sombre village crier,
    Ringing loud his brazen bell,
Wandered down the street proclaiming
    There was an estray to sell.

And the curious country people,
    Rich and poor, and young and old,
Came in haste to see this wondrous
    Winged steed, with mane of gold.

Thus the day passed, and the evening
    Fell, with vapours cold and dim;
But it brought no food nor shelter,
    Brought no straw nor stall, for him.

Patiently, and still expectant,
    Looked he through the wooden bars,
Saw the moon rise o'er the landscape,
    Saw the tranquil, patient stars;

Till at length, the bell at midnight
    Sounded from its dark abode,
And, from out a neighbouring farmyard,
    Loud the cock Alectryon crowed.

Then, with nostrils wide distended,
    Breaking from his iron chain,
And unfolding far his pinions,
    To those stars he soared again.

On the morrow, when the village
    Woke to all its toil and care,
Lo! the strange steed had departed,
    And they knew not when nor where.

But they found, upon the green-sward,
    Where his struggling hoofs had trod,
Pure and bright, a fountain flowing
    From the hoof-marks in the sod . . .

"Pegasus" HENRY WADSWORTH LONGFELLOW

When you are listening to stories, time seems to stand still; but now it is getting dark, night will come as swiftly as this poet sees her, walking over the sea from the caves where she has hidden all day, coming with her grey cloak and touching everyone with her wand, which makes them sleep:

Swiftly walk o'er the western wave,
    Spirit of Night!
Out of the misty eastern cave,
Where, all the long and lone daylight,
Thou wovest dreams of joy and fear,
Which make thee terrible and dear, –
    Swift be thy flight!

Wrap thy form in a mantle gray,
    Star-inwrought!
Blind with thine hair the eyes of Day;
Kiss her until she be wearied out,
Then wander o'er city, and sea, and land,
Touching all with thine opiate wand —
    Come, long-sought! . . .

"To Night" (extract) PERCY BYSSHE SHELLEY

"Star-inwrought" means woven with stars. "Opiate" means bringing sleep.

Have you ever thought that when you are in your bed,
your bed is in the room, and the room is in the house,
the house in the village or town, the town in, say,
England – or in America – England in Europe, both
in the Western hemisphere, the hemisphere in our earth,
earth in the universe and you, a little speck, are part
of it?

Supper in the boy, boy in his pyjamas,
Pyjamas in the bed, bed in the bedroom,
Bedroom in the mill-house, mill-house in the village,
Village near Cambridge, Cambridge in the county,
County in England, England in Europe,
      all at this moment lying under the moon.

Above, a Glorification of stars,
Below, a Veneration of grey hairs
And a Hope of little brothers and sisters,
And round about, left, right, and centre,
A Puzzle of extraordinary things,
      all at this moment lying under the moon.

"Collective Nouns" CHRISTOPHER HASSALL

In the Night

*Are you one of those children who does not like the
dark? (It used to fill me with terror.) Then there is no
bedtime poem more peaceful than this visionary one by
the poet William Blake, peaceful and reassuring, even
though wolves and tigers rush through it.*

*The animals are going to bed, not only in this world
but in the animals' heaven, where the killer and the
victim lie down together in forgiveness as friends – even
that unlikely pair, the lion and the lamb. Blake's lion
is splendid and resplendent, with his mane shining as it
has shone in this poem for more than two hundred years:*

The sun descending in the west,
The evening star does shine;
The birds are silent in their nest,
And I must seek for mine.
The moon like a flower
In heaven's high bower,
With silent delight
Sits and smiles on the night.

Farewell, green fields and happy groves,
Where flocks have took delight.
Where lambs have nibbled, silent moves
The feet of angels bright;
Unseen they pour blessing
And joy without ceasing,
On each bud and blossom,
And each sleeping bosom.

They look in every thoughtless nest,
Where birds are cover'd warm;
They visit caves of every beast,
To keep them all from harm.
If they see any weeping
That should have been sleeping,
They pour sleep on their head,
And sit down by their bed.

When wolves and tygers howl for prey,
They pitying stand and weep;
Seeking to drive their thirst away,
And keep them from the sheep;
But if they rush dreadful,
The angels, most heedful,
Receive each wild spirit,
New worlds to inherit.

And there the lion's ruddy eyes
Shall flow with tears of gold,
And pitying the tender cries,
And walking round the fold,
Saying "Wrath, by his meekness,
And by his health, sickness
is driven away
From our immortal day."

"And now beside thee, bleating lamb,
I can lie down and sleep;
Or think on him who bore thy name,
Graze after thee and weep.
For, wash'd in life's river,
My bright mane for ever
Shall shine like the gold
As I guard o'er the fold."

"Night" WILLIAM BLAKE

On fine nights there are always stars:

L ook at the stars! Look look up at the skies
O look at all the firefolk sitting in the air . . .

"The Starlight Night" (extract) GERARD MANLEY HOPKINS

S tarlight. Starbright.
First star I see tonight.
I wish I may, I wish I might
Have the wish I wish tonight.

"Star Wish" TRADITIONAL

O Lady Moon, your horns point towards the east:
              Shine, be increased;
O Lady Moon, your horns point towards the west:
              Wane, be at rest.

"Lady Moon" CHRISTINA ROSSETTI

The fairies sing a lullaby for Titania, their fairy queen:

You spotted snakes with double tongue,
    Thorny hedgehogs, be not seen;
  Newts and blind-worms, do no wrong,
    Come not near our fairy queen.

Philomel, with melody,
Sing in our sweet lullaby;
Lulla, lulla, lullaby; lulla, lulla, lullaby:
Never harm,
Nor spell, nor charm,
Come our lovely lady nigh;
So, good night, with lullaby.

Weaving spiders, come not here;
Hence, you long-legg'd spinners, hence!
Beetles black, approach not near;
Worm nor snail, do no offence

Philomel, with melody,
Sing in our sweet lullaby;
Lulla, lulla, lullaby; lulla, lulla, lullaby:
Never harm,
Nor spell, nor charm,
Come our lovely lady nigh;
So, good night, with lullaby.

"Fairies' Lullaby for Titania" WILLIAM SHAKESPEARE

"Philomel" is the nightingale. When the poet says "snakes with double tongue" it is because snakes' tongues are forked.

*A different sort of lullaby. Nokomis was a Native
American grandmother. Hiawatha, who grew up to be a
great warrior, was her baby grandson:*

By the shores of Gitche Gumee
By the shining Big-Sea-Water,
Stood the wigwam of Nokomis,
Daughter of the Moon, Nokomis,
Dark behind it rose the forest,
Rose the black and gloomy pine-trees,
Rose the firs with cones upon them;
Bright before it beat the water,
Beat the clear and sunny water,
Beat the shining Big-Sea-Water.

There the wrinkled, old Nokomis
Nursed the little Hiawatha,
Rocked him in his linden cradle,
Bedded soft in moss and rushes,
Safely bound with reindeer sinews;
Stilled his fretful wail by saying,
"Hush! the Naked Bear will hear thee!"
Lulled him into slumber, singing,
"Ewa-yea! my little owlet!"
Who is this, that light the wigwam?
With his great eyes lights the wigwam?
"Ewa-yea! my little owlet!"

Many things Nokomis taught him
Of the stars that shine in heaven;
Showed him Ishkoodah, the comet,
Ishkoodah, with fiery tresses;
Showed the Death-Dance of the spirits,
Warriors with their plumes and war-clubs,
Flaring far away to northward
In the frosty nights of Winter . . .

    Saw the moon rise from the water
Rippling, rounding from the water,
Saw the flecks and shadows on it,
Whispered, "What is that, Nokomis?"
And the good Nokomis answered:
"Once a warrior, very angry,
Seized his grandmother, and threw her
Up into the sky at midnight;
Right against the moon he threw her;
'Tis her body that you see there" . . .

"Hiawatha's Childhood" (extract)
HENRY WADSWORTH LONGFELLOW

Moonlight is said to make you light-headed and frivolous and cheeky, like this little dressed-up girl:

She was wearing the coral taffeta trousers
Someone had brought her from Isfahan,
And the little gold coat with pomegranate blossoms,
And the coral-hafted feather fan;
But she ran down a Kentish lane in the moonlight,
And skipped in the pool of the moon as she ran.

She cared not a rap for all the big planets,
For Betelgeuse or Alderbaran,
And all the big planets cared nothing for her,
That small impertinent charlatan,
As she climbed on a Kentish stile in the moonlight,
And laughed at the sky through the sticks of her fan.

"Full Moon" VITA SACKVILLE-WEST

The moon has set,
The Seven Stars have set as well:
It is the middle of the night,
The hour goes by,
And by myself I lie.

"The Moon has Set" SAPPHO

And another alone poem:

I have been one acquainted with the night.
I have walked out in rain – and back in rain.
I have outwalked the furthest city light.

I have looked down the saddest city lane.
I have passed by the watchman on his beat
And dropped my eyes, unwilling to explain.

I have stood still and stopped the sound of feet
When far away an interrupted cry
Came over houses from another street,

But not to call me back to say good-bye;
And further still at an unearthly height,
One luminary clock against the sky
Proclaimed the time was neither wrong nor right.
I have been one acquainted with the night.

"Acquainted with the Night" ROBERT FROST

*That is a lonely poem, yet all the time, from midnight till
dawn, there are some creatures who do not sleep, and
make small rustlings and trippings – and trottings:*

Madame Mouse trots,
Grey in the black night!
Madame Mouse trots:
Furred is the light.
The elephant-trunks
Trumpet from the sea . . .

Grey in the black night
The mouse trots free.
Hoarse as a dog's bark
The heavy leaves are furled . . .
The cat's in his cradle,
All's well with the world!

"Madame Mouse" EDITH SITWELL

But not all cats are in their cradles:

Jellicle Cats come out to-night
Jellicle Cats come one come all:
The Jellicle Moon is shining bright –
Jellicles come to the Jellicle Ball.
Jellicle Cats are black and white,
Jellicle Cats are rather small;
Jellicle Cats are merry and bright,
And pleasant to hear when they caterwaul.
Jellicle Cats have cheerful faces,
Jellicle Cats have bright black eyes;
They like to practise their airs and graces
And wait for the Jellicle Moon to rise.

Jellicle Cats develop slowly,
Jellicle Cats are not too big;
Jellicle Cats are roly-poly,
They know how to dance a gavotte and a jig.
Until the Jellicle Moon appears
They make their toilette and take their repose:
Jellicles wash behind their ears,
Jellicles dry between their toes.

Jellicle Cats are white and black,
Jellicle Cats are of moderate size;
Jellicles jump like a jumping-jack,
Jellicle Cats have moonlit eyes.
They're quiet enough in the afternoon,
Reserving their terpsichorean powers
To dance by the light of the Jellicle Moon.

Jellicle Cats are black and white,
Jellicle Cats (as I said) are small;
If it happens to be a stormy night
They will practise a caper or two in the hall.
If it happens the sun is shining bright
You would say they had nothing to do at all:
They are resting and saving themselves to be right
For the Jellicle Moon and the Jellicle Ball.

"The Song of the Jellicles" T. S. ELIOT

"Terpsichore" is the Muse of Dancing.

All through "The Song of the Jellicles" you can hear the tripping and running of those cats' feet: so light, so neat, in their caperings, they make hardly any noise. But now the ball is over; the stars pale, dawn begins in the East, cocklight, and, sure enough, soon a clarion call breaks the stillness:

D o not forget, Lord,
it is I who make the sun rise.
I am Your servant
but, with the dignity of my calling,
I need some glitter and ostentation.
Noblesse oblige . . .
All the same,
I am Your servant,
only . . . do not forget, Lord,
I make the sun rise.

"The Prayer of the Cock" CARMEN BERNOS DE GASZTOLD
  Translator: Rumer Godden

Index of First Lines

A little Saint best fits a little Shrine   82

After the children left it, after it stood   73

All things that love the sun are out of doors   21

Allie, call the birds in   75

Alone, and stirring lightly in the night   67

Ann, Ann!   20

As gardens grow with flowers   26

Beautiful soup, so rich and green   81

But the Queen of Sheba went with Solomon   100

By the shores of Gitche Gumee   112

Children born of fairy stock   10

Do not forget, Lord   3, 118

Do you need a cabin boy?   45

Drum on your drums, batter on your banjos   31

Every Thursday morning   4

First paint a cage   52

Girls scream   62

Half the time they munched the grass   14

Hibou et Minou allèrent à la mer   59

I am called Childhood, in play is all my mind   46

I am cold and alone   72

I cling and swing   7

I had a little nut-tree, nothing would it bear   32

I have been one acquainted with the night.   115

I'll tell you how the sun rose   3

I'm Nobody! Who are you?	29
In this world a tablecloth need not be laid	79
Isabel met an enormous bear	95
It's a very odd thing	38
It will not do, I must go in	83
Jellicle Cats come out to-night	116
Jesse James was a two-gun man	69
Just look at him! There he stands	9
Laura's new this year in school	42
Lily Smith, tall and slender	40
Little Orphant Annie came to our house to stay	94
Look at the stars! Look look up at the skies	109
Madame Mouse trots	115
Mind your own business	40
Minnie and Winnie	6
Needles and ribbons and packets of pins	50
Nine o'Clock Bell!	22
Now I'm really, really extremely tired	54
Nymph, nymph, what are your beads?	97
O Lady Moon, your horns point towards the east	110
On Monday, Monday	42
Once into a quiet village	101
Once more he stept into the street	33
Once when the snow of the year was beginning to fall	71
Out of the paper bag	37
Piping down the valleys wild	25
Roses are red	41
She was wearing the coral taffeta trousers	114
Starlight. Starbright.	109

Sunlight, moonlight	93
Supper in the boy, boy in his pyjamas	104
Swiftly, walk o'er the western wave	103
Tattle tale, tattle tale	40
The King asked	15
The moon has set	114
The Owl and the Pussy-Cat went to sea	60
The rain has silver sandals	21
The shadows flickering, the daylight dying.	89
The sun descending in the west	107
The year's at the spring	10
There is walk-in-Park-on-lead.	84
There was a boy of other days	30
There was also a Nun, a Prioress	19
They were not lonely. They found the sea	57
Things men have made with wakened hands	51
This is the day for bicycles.	65
This is the night mail crossing the border	4
Thou mak'st my teeming Hen to lay	13
Three gypsies stood at the Castle gate	98
Twas only at Llewelyn's board	85
Two and two four	27
Under the greenwood tree	44
We had two little guinea pigs	88
When bread-and-cheese	39
When I was but thirteen or so	55
Whistle! A kick! A rush, a scramble, a scrum	49
You can't catch me!	67
You spotted snakes with double tongue	110

Acknowledgements

The compiler and publisher would like to thank the following
for permission to reprint the selections in this book.
All possible care has been taken to trace the ownership of every
work included and to make full acknowledgement for its use.
If any errors or omissions have accidentally occurred, they will
be corrected in subsequent editions, provided notification is
sent to the publishers.

The Post Office for 'Night Mail' by W. H. Auden.

Sarah Matthews for 'Chips' by Stanley Cook.

The Estate of W. H. Davies for 'School's Out' by W. H. Davies,
published by Jonathan Cape. Reprinted by permission of Random
Century Group.

Faber and Faber Ltd. for 'The Song of the Jellicles' by T. S. Eliot from
Old Possum's Book of Practical Cats.

David Higham Associates for 'Nine-O'Clock Bell', 'Words' and
'Catch' by Eleanor Farjeon.

The Estate of Robert Frost for 'The Runaway' and 'Acquainted with
the Night' by Robert Frost from *The Poetry of Robert Frost*, published by
Jonathan Cape. Reprinted by permission of the Random Century Group.

A. P. Watt Ltd. on behalf of The Trustees of the Robert Graves
Copyright Trust for 'I'd Love to be a Fairy's Child' by Robert Graves
taken from *Fairies and Fusiliers* and for 'Allie' taken from *Collected
Poems 1975*.

Aitken & Stone Ltd. for 'One Star Less' by Russell Hoban.

James Kirkup for 'Tea in a Space Ship' by James Kirkup from *The
Prodigal Son*.

Laurence Pollinger Ltd. and the Estate of Frieda Lawrence Ravagli
for 'Things Men Have Made' by D. H. Lawrence.

The Literary Trustees of Walter de la Mare and the Society of Authors as their representative for 'Alas! Alack!', 'Miss T.', and 'Dream Song' by Walter de la Mare.

R.I.B. Library for 'The King's Breakfast' by A. A. Milne from *When We Were Very Young*, published by Methuen Children's Books.

Bantam Books, a division of Bantam Doubleday Dell Publishing Group, Inc. for 'Laura' by Jeff Moss from *The Butterfly Jar*. Copyright © 1989 Jeff Moss.

Little, Brown and Company for 'Adventures of Isabel' by Ogden Nash from *Bad Parents' Garden of Verses*. Copyright © 1936 Ogden Nash.

Laura Cecil Literary Agency for 'Cows' by James Reeves from *The Wandering Moon and Other Poems* (Puffin Books). Reprinted by permission of the James Reeves Estate.

Curtis Brown, London, on behalf of the author's estate for 'Full Moon' by Vita Sackville-West.

David Higham Associates for 'The Dustman' by Clive Samson from *The Golden Unicorn*, published by Methuen.

Harcourt Brace & Company for 'Jazz Fantasia' by Carl Sandberg.

Ian Serraillier for 'The Ballad of Kon-Tiki' from *Across the Pacific*.

David Higham Associates for 'Madame Mouse' by Edith Sitwell from *Collected Poems 1936*.

James Sutherland for 'Computer'.

Mrs A. M. Walsh for 'Skipping Song' by John Walsh from *The Roundabout by the Sea* published by Oxford University Press.

The playground rhymes come from *The Lore and Language of School Children* by Iona and Peter Opie.

A selected list of poetry books available from Macmillan

The prices shown below are correct at the time of going to press. However, Macmillan Publishers reserve the right to show new retail prices on covers which may differ from those previously advertised.

Cockcrow to Starlight
Edited by Rumer Godden
0 330 34265 7
£4.99

Selected Poems for Children
Charles Causley
0 330 35404 3
£5.99

A Spell of Words
Elizabeth Jennings
0 330 35422 1
£4.99

Glitter When You Jump
Edited by Fiona Waters
0 330 34104 9
£3.99

One of Your Legs is Both the Same
Henri, Jones, Rosen, Wright & McNaughton
0 330 32704 6
£3.99

Another Day on Your Foot and I Would Have Died
Agard, Cope, McGough, Mitchell & Patten
0 330 34048 4
£3.99

We Couldn't Provide Fish Thumbs
Berry, Nicholls, Nichols, Scannell & Sweeney
0 330 35236 9
£3.99

All Macmillan titles can be ordered at your local bookshop or are available by post from:

**Book Service by Post
PO Box 29, Douglas, Isle of Man IM99 1BQ**

Credit cards accepted. For details:
Telephone: 01624 675137
Fax: 01624 670923
E-mail: bookshop@enterprise.net

Free postage and packing in the UK.
Overseas customers: add £1 per book (paperback) and £3 per book (hardback).